You Never Marry Your Muse:
Prose Work and Supposed Poetry

Brooklynn DeVours

Brooklynn Dean
PO Box 13
Chalk Hill, PA 15421

www.brooklynndean.com

Dedication

Though you'll find many contemplations centered around my muses—those existing in this realm with me, and those in far-off planes—I cannot dedicate this book to any of them.

Certainly not my nearest one, who has been written into more of my works than necessary. To him, I say this: I adore you, and I'm sorry about that time I killed you, and for everything else I've done to you while imagining who you might be, and for everything I've done to you while learning who you are. I've written enough words for you. I have plenty more. But this book is not for you. This book is not for my muse, the muse, muses at large.

Instead, I dedicate this book to gods. To the divine creations who have, themselves, become creators.

I dedicate this book, more specifically, to the gods of my own pantheon. To A. To E. The masters of language, of poetics, of prose.

I am god to those I create. I've said it before; I will continue saying it. But to pass into this world another hallucinatory, filleted corpse of once-living flora now riddled with the symbology of man in some pattern that can project my inner-workings into you, dear reader, into your mind, without acknowledging the greats who have paved this path of human connectivity to me would be arrogant and absurd.

A, E,
Thank you for your love of language. Thank you for extending yourselves to me the way I extend myself to strangers now.

To the Creators, the Creatives, the Mortal Gods,
Consume me. Let me inside you.
    -Brooklynn DeVours

You Never Marry Your Muse:
Prose Work and Supposed Poetry

Brooklynn DeVours

The First Born

I was born a snake
In the Garden of Man
With my tongue I spat venom
While they attempted to stand
I whispered my lies
So appealing to them
That they knelt at my belly
Gasping 'Amen'
I slithered up their necks
Wrapped my body 'round their throats
Injected them with poison
Hidden in musical notes
Replaced their blood with acid
Laced into what I wrote
Masquerading as a monster
I bore witness to their fall
When they praised me as their Master
I called them Puppet and Doll
When they realized they had sinned
I laughed, for I had caused it all

Poem I

I've got an angel at my throat
And Christ wrapped around my finger
He's crucified inside my trunk
Outside I see him linger

The angel grabs at me
He slips in my veins
Replacing oxygen with alchemy
And bleeds inside my brain

I've been to heaven and back
I tell him I prefer hell
The angel becomes demons
Book, candle, and bell

And every time I move
I feel the spear of destiny
Stabbing into my side
Forcing me to breathe

Exhaling from my body
All the bone and brain matter
That makes hallucinations tangible
Writing words in the blood spatter

Transferring the images
Into the minds
Of all those who see me
When they read between the lines

Breathe in my saving blasphemy
Let my words seep in your soul
Like only the Holy Ghost can do
When the funeral bells softly toll

Praise

Ignorance is bliss
And lies are pretty prose
He absorbs the surface phrasing
But in his mind he knows
My baptism isn't meant to be sweet
That it's smarter to worship me
Before floor and knees meet
He embraces his natural status
As the weaker of the sexes
Falling into his birthright's position
Genuflecting to offer respect
To someone else's religion
Enjoying the affliction
Of every crucifixion
Offered by this god
Of blood and moon and Venus
Absorbing each blow of the rod
As he relinquishes his freeness
Taking in the soul
Breathing, gasping
A singular extol
To the woman risen
Standing towering
In flesh, the apparition
Ghosts of past and present
Flickering in the face
Of what exists before him
Above him

Inflicting painful grace
Upon this new supplicant
On his knees
In a silken prison
I bruise the skin
To purify the spirit
Releasing with the flowing blood
Everyone who had been near it
He must release these beings
From his bones and from his brain
In order to be my prized possession
Inside the depths of my domain
When his back is broken
By tears throughout the skin
Rise, the whispered word is spoken
And he obeys, stands,
Lowers his chin
Extends his wrists
Ready for the chains
I lock him in
Urge him on
He lies in velvet shame
Opens his fingers
Revealing palms
Ready to be nailed down
Above the binds
That make his wrists red and raw
Double the pain
Increase the pleasure
Because his healer

Is also his oppressor
When the surface of his flesh
Is smooth and whole again
No one will have touched the skin
But me,
his replacement god
Blessed be
Amen

Blues and Bruises

I pin him down
His wrists over his head
I pound nails into his palms
Which open
Fingers unfurling
Lazily languidly
His teeth press into his lip
His eyes glaze
Hooded
Fluttering between
Open and closed
He's edging
Because
The skin of my teeth
Was never my own

Poem VI

Sitting in the darkness
I stare at pictures of angels carved in stone
I wonder if the entities they represent
Fall to earth and call these statues home
Imagine walking through the cemetery gates
And seeing a marble angel atop a gravestone
Unfurling its concrete wings
The stone would grind against itself
Crumbling as the tendons stretched
Feather shaped gravel plummeting to earth
Which shook beneath the moving feet of
possessed pillars
What would those pupil-less eyes see
When they blinked open from downcast heads
When the necks would snap in landslides
When the fingertips broke through the atmosphere
Paralyzed I'd stand on the asphalt path
Watching lightning encase itself in man made
visages
Imposed upon the endless cosmos collected into
wheels and wings
Harken! The stone angels would bellow but I'd
hear not a sound
The artist gave them only surface
To exterior they're bound
No vocal chords to shake the smoothened throat
You're trapped I'd say watching them reach to their
necks

Marble nails crumble as they dig at the concrete
flesh
Fingertips fall away
You are not the stone I'd say you are the soul
Which animates already this flesh
Come into me if you cannot return heavenward
Take this skin and these lips and these languages
Call my body your home
And the angel would animate the stone
Stepping down from the concrete pillars and odes
And the crumbling fingers would find me now
And I'd inhale gravel and stone
And the angel would possess me
And call this body home

A Ballad for Galahad: Muse A1

His unruly brows
Never match the color of his hair
He's chaos and disorder
Wrapped in purity and prayer

When he blinks there's only skin
Covering the blues and greens
That run like rivers to the surface
Of galaxies unseen

He cannot be discovered
He reveals what keeps him clean
Even though he's hiding poetry
Within the blatantly obscene

His lies roll off his serpent's tongue
To cover the despair
Lying dormant in the lovesick
Lyrics written on a Dare

Everything he does is magic
An alchemist at heart
He even the sound of laughter
Turns to tears within his art

His blood is crushed up petals
Of the softest Violet tones

His tears are frigid forests
Trapped eternally in Globes

He falls apart in silence
When the melody subsides
And opens up his spirit
To every tear he's cried

He breeds with sorrow in the sadness
He propagates the pain
So when he paints it into music
He turns it into fame

He's depth and darkness masquerading
As every colored hue
Of the upbeat base experience
Of all he can't subdue

He goes to Sleep Alone
He crumbles to the floor
While we scream in through the windows
And we work to break the door

If he's half the soul he seems to be
Then this message won't suffice
For much more than a crumpled ball
Of loss, and lust, and vice

So take your syntax and your songs
And press your fingers to the neck

Giving only what you want to give
Instead of time and blood and sweat

His pain is not for profit
Unless he wants to pay the price
But pain can be his savior
If he wants to roll the dice

We breathe him in our lungs
Instead of leaning into sin
We can see the cherub singing
Inside his handsome skin

The devil wears the crown
Of a very pretty prince
He seduces and he charms
With the weaponry of lips

He uses all his beauty
To shield his sword from our sharp sight
For angels dance with demons
Inside the heart of a brave and broken
Dark Knight

Poem XI

Glitter dances along your face
Ascending up the bone
Buried within your flesh
Where only blood should roam

Salt-soaked red smears down your lip
Across the side of your chin
Where the creamy skin wraps tautly
Around the deadly jaw within

And when you open up your mouth
Expelling gasps and moans
The soul rolls off your tongue
In melody and tones

You sing in duality
All sanctified and sin
Gasping out your blasphemy
In a voice befitting hymns

And when you wrap the chains
Of rebellion at your throat
Around your forming fists
You cry out what you wrote

The visual becomes a sound
Your voice becomes a hope

For everyone beneath you
Gazing upward to their pope

You denounce the very god
You keep buried in your chest
You drink the air from bottles
You're too saintly to ingest

And everyone beneath you
Reaching for a platform from the floor
Worships the part you play
While your soul go unadored

I want to worship you in ways
You never wanted known
So that when you wipe away your makeup
You see only flesh and bone

I want to taste the salt
Slipping down your sweat soaked chest
To breathe in from your lips
What your heaving lungs reject

Give me your face when it's clean
Give me the tainted soul within
I want to devour you in darkness
So you can be born again

And when you rise tomorrow
Velvet purring at your skin

Remember how adored you were
In rubbed-raw flesh and tender sin

You needn't wrap the spikes or chains
Around your wrists and at your neck
No threat of injury will keep me
From this doting disrespect

You are not the villain
Not the hero you adore
You're a flesh-bound angel
Trapped in a world of a metaphor

So blink your brilliant blues
And sing your wounded song
And know that I will be here
To cage you when you've gone

Repeating

He gasps
And he grunts
He groans
Voice crying out
in moans
As blood from his bite
Drips with the spit
Falling from his lips
As he recites
The pleas of his pleasure
Gasps of delight
In the pain of this plight

Praises and prayers
Blend screams with sighs
He does not want it to end
He wails as tears spill from his eyes
As the warmth in his gut
Ignites flames in his thighs

I yank them together
Pinning them down
Tethered
By another nail
In his coffin of silk
His confessions of guilt
Spurring me forth
To destroy what he'd built

To conquer the spirit
Inside his skin
By bruising it
Cream colored flesh
Growing purple and green
Erasing from his mind's eyes
All it had seen
Prior to his entry
To this sacred space of sin
He'd bow before me
If he were loosened again

But I cannot breathe freely
With the life in him growing
He's got to succumb
To be released from this sowing
He's reaping
He's repentant
His sentence is ongoing

Mean it I whisper
You must mean what you say
He worships
He praises
But his words are delayed
He can't help but moan
He cries out in satisfaction
It's not time I tell him
To complete this connection

Withdrawing from him
All the latex and chains
I remind him his completion
Is not the goal of this game
Though the body is his
It is all my domain
He cannot decide to participate
To play or abstain
The satin of this realm
Is controlled by my reign

He protests in vain
Eyes blinking in lust
His role in the play
Is one of distrust

But no special word
Uttered by his lips
Provides all the evidence
Of his compliance
With this

The savior splayed open
Displayed
In my bed
An unwilling participant
Of all he desires and dreads

He's warmed and he's wetted
He's hydrated and fed

Too happy to be suffering
Too healthy to be dead

I take his life slowly
Gradually
He fades into the abyss
Of unconsciousness
Of repose
Of the gentle sleep
I impose

And when he awakes
The holes will remain
He'll be sticky with sweat
Traces of blood in his brain

Memory ignites
He remembers the crucifixion
Of two bodies
In satin
And velvet
And affectionate affliction

Mortal
Prose Work 72

He lies in the bed next to me. A faint smile still
lingering on his lips. They're drying, and cracking;
small pieces of blanched skin dotting the pink of
his lower lip. The circles of death still attached at
their center points to the living being; edges curling
upward, graying, frayed.
Sometimes his lips are smooth and creamy. They're
moistened. Dewy. All lively and warm and wet.
And, even then, while lying in this bed, I see the
signs of death upon his handsome face.
It's got nothing to do with his slumbering body; the
eyes closed in sleep—a fraction of death. The
moonlight cascades into the room, as it always does,
painting his tanned skin in silvery tones. Silver so
close to gray. Gray. Like death. Clammy skin.
Clammy and white. Drained of blood.
The veins and vessels so obvious beneath the
opaque skin. Their canals caked with coagulated
blood. But nothing flows through them.
The heart cages by bones does not beat. All will
soon deteriorate but those ribs, but that skull.
I hear him breathing, but I imagine him still. I see
the skin slipping away from his forehead, falling
into lumps of slimy flesh on the ground, in the bed,
sticking to the silk beneath his face. It falls from his
high cheekbones. The tip of his nose blackens; I
see it crumbling away.

The brilliant blues of his irises are eaten by worms. Maggots wriggle from their eggs inside his brain. That brain, the home of his mind, unlike the home of his heart—his rib cage—for even it will not remain. It will soften. Rot away. Taking with its decay all the sparks of personality, the talent, the depth of his emotion, the intelligence. Every word he's ever spoke, gone. Every sensation ever felt, lost forever.

Someone will dig into the earth, and place a box inside the hole. His decaying flesh inside it. In another satin home.

I wonder if I'll be there. If I'll stand above the grave, tears slipping from my eyes, hidden by black frames.

Or will I have left before him. Will I rot away before he dies? And if I go first into that eternal night, will he stand above me and cry?

He's existed long before me, so I imagine I'll make-up the difference when he dies. And I hate to think about it, especially here in this bed as he sleeps so peacefully beside me.

But the traces of gray already invade his dark hair. And the lines of his laughter remain upon his skin. He will not stay this way forever. No one of us will. And while most lovers see their future in visions of intimacy, commitment, and growth, I gaze at my divine masculine and see only his mortality.

I want to flee. As always, I see them dying, and it inspires me to run away.

I'd rather leave while they're still living, so I hate them far before they die away.
But this one. Something different. Something magnetic about his frame. It draws me closer, guides me near, asks me to hold him where he lies. I comply, another unusual experience for me and my brain, and I feel him stir and stretch and sigh. He doesn't open his eyes, but he smiles, and opens up to me. His arm slips around my shoulders, calls me into his embrace. He whispers how warm he feels with me, and says it's got nothing to do with body heat.
It's all spirit, he says, confirming what I've already felt.
And while I hold him, kissing his cheek as he slips back into sleep, away from conscious thought, all I can think of is the inevitability that, someday, he will die.

Please Stop/Please Don't:
Prose Work II

Sometimes it feels powerful to curse something
good. To hurt something tender. To corrupt
something pure.
Perhaps it's because he's so pretty when his elegant
features contort pleasure into pain; when his brows
furrow, eyes squeezing closed, plump lips panting,
gasping, moaning.
When he looks up and says, "please," it's as
arousing when its followed by "stop" as "don't
stop."
He licks his lips, tastes iron and salt. But he loves
his own destruction. Loves that it's not his fault.
He delights in the supplication; becomes more
himself as he follows each command.
It's so beautiful to hear him beg, when he asks to
keep going, to stop, when he knows I ignore it,
ignoring him. He likes to keep his innocence so I
take anything I can.

Lessons Learned

I can't breathe
He whispers
And I say
That's got nothing to do with me

Blunt nails drag along opaque hose
Serrating the skin as the fabric runs
Punctuated wounds form beneath fingertips

Try harder, I tell him
Try to run
But he disobeys
As his eyes oblige
A duality of the dominance
He never wanted
But is expected to exert

Come into my strangling embrace
Let me suffocate the expectation out of you
Give you back your natural state
Riddle me with violence
So I can wear the scars you create
A symbol of my power
For I overcome
And I leave pressed upon you
Those same symbols

Bearing to the world
That you succumb

Out and About

I keep him in mason jars
Spread about the bathroom
On tile floors he lies
Creamy over pink
His lips are always parted
Brows are hinting at expression
He's too vivid to be stagnant
Even when he's motionless
His chest is always heaving
As if he cannot catch his breath
And when he blinks it's elegant
As if he can't see past his chest
The blue irises glaze
An arm bent, hand near his head
The other lies upon his stomach
Its fingers loose and spread
What are you doing
Comes the gentle easy tone
Half groggy from the exertion
Of affection
And drooling
From the languid pace
Of auto asphyxiation
The oxygen depletes in time
Inside his chest and mind
The brain and heart still functioning
The soul becoming unaligned
As his dizziness increases

His inhibition plummets
His body statuesque
Immobile yes
But perfected too
And fixed now to the floor
Ceramic tiles cool his skin
As neurons fire off
Don't tell me what you'll do, he says
Just say you love me
When I wake up

Fingerprints

Your blunt nails trace
Words into my flesh
The fleshy sensation
Of invisible letters
Overpowers the permanence
Of similar sentiments
Inked into my skin
Your unseen prose
Runs deeper than flesh
It slips into my pores
Pulling your essence
Along with its script
Deep inside of me
I feel you entering my veins
Your spirit following the vessels
Infusing with the blood
Riding its current
Into my unused organ
Cold and closed off and concealed
Until your touch ignites the skin
Burning my circulatory system
With your passion
With your poetry
I am thawing
I am warmed
My body is spring anew
Where my soul had been lingering

In an eternal winter
Awaiting you

His Attractive Trauma Responses

I always loved the way
You sit upon your hands.
Adore they way you blush
At compliments unplanned.
I love the way you bow your head
When you think yourself unseen.
The concern you hold for others
In times of personal need.

Then I met a woman
Hurt and healed and so attuned,
Who told me everything I love in you
Grew out of some horrific wound.

She told me of responses
Risen out of fear
That trauma of the distant past
Is always very near

I hate to think of your soft spirit
Your tender, delicate charm
As learned behavior from
Some repeated harm

I've seen the strength in your arms
But saw meekness in your soul
And now I see how wrong I was
To think you aren't the strongest man I know

I can't heal your wounds
Can't save you from your past
But I can ensure tomorrow and all that follows
And that you've found safety at last

BWGT

Infinity's embedded in his skin
Electricity upon his tongue
Its shockwaves burst with serotonin
As words rise up from his lungs
The oceans inside his eyes
Are salted by the implication
Of countless metaphoric lies
Turned true through contemplation
And every time he tries to breathe
His ribs give way to meter
So even as he tries to leave
He's pulled down ever deeper
I feel the vellum of his moldy soul
When I press my hands against his chest
Its residue left on the manifested symbol
Of the consumption he'll infest
As blood pools around my fingers
Through a barrier of flesh
The intellect still lingers
Inside his weaker sex
I want to taste the bubble gum
Of his candied brain
Pulling from the cerebellum
Every thought he can't explain
Instinct conquers consciousness
Words fight the gasping moans
Pretentious proseworks acquiesce
To unintelligible odes

I suffocate in exhales
Drowning in the sound
I breathe in everything he said
He never meant to tell
Awareness battles instinct
Words fight the gasping moans
The flow of his cadence linked
With unintelligible odes
I want to press my tongue against his brain
And taste the flavor of his thoughts
I want to suffocate him in syntax
Find rapture in his rot
Resurrect him
Disrespect him
Finding freedom
In the cost
Baptize him
Chastise him
Find affection
In the fault

Pretty Bones

Monster were never monstrous
That's how they slip inside
Creep in your mind
Steal your heart
And devour your soul
No need to manipulate
To steal or to take
You give it freely
When you wake from nightmares
At three a.m. and you see
A shadowy frame in the corner of your space
Sweat beading on your forehead
Worry animating your face
But when the figure steps forward
Relief replaces the fear
Calms the increased rate of your heart's pace
As it moves near
Pretty bones
Gleaming eyes
They're blue
Paired with blonde hair
And red lips that smile at you
So blinded by the affection
Your brain does register
The dangers of the sharpened incisors
Your eyes can perceive
Even as they tear into your flesh
Ripping it away in chunks

Then pulling it into the lips
That were pressed against yours
Then your jaw then your neck
Then wrap around your shoulder
Embracing you softly before colliding
The two frames mangled in an amorous wreckage
Closing tightly at your body with lips and with hands
Leaving bruises in the shape of my prints
Like stars riddling the sky of your skin
Sucking the lifeforce from within
Drawing your blood into my spirit
While infecting you with pleasures
Embedded in the spit
Stigmata forms within the palms
Decorated with faux leather
Bleeding out the open wounds
All the pain of this love letter
I bandage you and bind you
I move slowly while behind you
And you won't forget
What's come to pass
The scars will constantly remind you
Close your eyes
I'll wipe your tears
Fall into nightmares
Full of fears
And when you rise
Once you wake
You'll know your soul
Was mine to take

Muse A2: The Softest Inspiration

I suck the sour off of candy
And spit the sweetness on his tongue
He swallows the sugar and salvia
While I split my own in two
Swiping the fork over my lips
Wetting them for him
So when he leans into me
He doesn't taste the venom
I inject into him

King is Second; Queen is God:
Prose Work I

If he thinks she's not the villain, she instructed him
that way. Her aggression is most obvious when it's
not expressed in his direction.
She knows when it comes to him that subtly will
reign, for no almighty prince or king bows willingly
to anything.
He watches her as she aggresses, as she stands her
ground, brawls. He watches as her loosened hands
curl into tightened fists. If he'd see her thrust one
forward, he'd be as horrified as aroused.
The king is mighty, yes, but only in the
masquerade.

Poem II

You are not used to being owned
But you cannot exist freely with me

Bare your throat
Let me inside

I want to feel your flesh press into memory,
The nerve-endings respond with the mind

Your scent morph into sound,
Your body heat life giving sun,

Every tear where I can drown

Every thought becomes a whisper,

Every inch becomes an ocean

I want to waste away inside the daydream of your
sensuous distress,
I want to hear you gasp as I tightened my grasp,
Around your neck

I want to feel your flesh press into memory,
The sparks of home in your soul

Find it between my thighs
So that sorrow

                    You Never Marry

Slips away from your hand
When it falls from your eyes

You never have to feel unwanted
When you feel me holding tight
The strength of my constrictive fingers
The heat of my gaslight

I want to feel your flesh press into memory,
Embedded in my brain

Come into my embrace
Forget the life you've lived
And remember the present with me

I want to feel your flesh
Press into memory

August End

He's loud and sociable
And I'm loud and a loner
I can only make him shut up
When he's gasping and groaning
But still he expresses
Every sensation he feels
I want to press my palm against his lips
And make him shudder and reel
I want his heels to dig into the mattress
As I dig into his skin
I want his wrists to rub against his binds
Until the flesh is torn and thin
I'll laugh at his whimpers
As I taste his throat
Blood pools beneath its surface
A painful antidote
He wants to hurt as much or more
As I want to inflict my force
He wants to feel the burning sting
Of every bloody course
I craft into his skin
All the paths of my advantage
So when it's over he'll feel relief
From every remembered damage
His heart housed wounds
His persona was too exuberant to feel
But in the darkness of my silk and satin
His intellect becomes only sex appeal

So let your gasps replace the words
You so poetically express
Submit to me in silence
All the pain that you suppress
You need not hide behind
The character crafted in your mind
Reveal to me your basic id
I'll conquer you with mine.

1974 : Art is Born : Muse M2
Prose Work III

I write endlessly for men who mean little more to
me than their faces.
I never write about yours.
I realized I can't turn you into art. You're already
poetry.
No font is perfect enough to symbolize your
language; no language lovely enough to articulate
you.
I can't perceive your meter. You have no obvious
melody.
But within your every motion, every musing, you
are elegant, entrancing.
How do I immortalize you? How do I describe you?
How do I love you?
I don't think it's possible—not for me, but for
anyone. You're too perfect to love properly. We are
fallible, you are not.

I See You

I See You

You look so pretty
When you think no one is watching you
I love to watch you move
When you think no one is watching you
Your smiles slips away
When you think no one is watching you
You lower your chin
When you think no one is watching you
Your eyes fall, too
When you think no one is watching you
Your shoulders curve in
When you think no one is watching you
The mask slips away
When you think no one is watching you
Laughter becomes pain
When you think no one is watching you
The gleam in your eyes falls away
When you think no one is watching you

You always have an audience
When you think no one is watching you
But you don't want to be seen
When you think no one is watching you

I bear witness
When you think no one is watching you

Stand with me
When no one is watching you
Follow me to the door
When no one is watching you
Remove your layers
When no one is watching you
Slip into the sheets
When no one is watching you
Don't stifle your breath
When no one is watching you

I'll watch you enter
When I'm the only one watching you
I'll lock the door
When I'm the only one watching you
I'll pull the blinds
When I'm the only one watching you

Melt into me
When we're the only ones watching us

Feel my eyes
When you think no one is watching you
I bear witness
When you think no one is watching you
I see beyond the facade
When you think no one is watching you
Look over to me
When you think no one is watching you

See my gaze fixate
When you think no one is watching you

A Creator and A Realized Dream: Poem VIII

I am an author at random,
A poet at heart,
The pen is my sword,
The words are my art.
I'll paint you prose work,
Then erase your humanity,
You're an extension of my musings,
A breathing fantasy.
Let me hold you, an angel,
By the wings in your back,
Let the agony enfold you,
As they break and they snap.
Become the realization,
Of every illusion,
Define so distinctly,
What once was allusion.
When we let your veins,
What will spill from the wounds,
Your life force isn't blood,
But a meter and tunes.
When your soul expresses,
From your gasping lips,
Let me chalice the bleeding,
Drink the communion of hips.
Your soul can't be your body,
For neither feels real,
You are art already,
Absurdist and surreal.

At least when I touch you,
The memory remains,
So, if we are not soul,
We surely are brains.
What is the flesh without the sin of it,
The skin without the mind,
The living poet is art already;
I cannot turn him into rhyme.

Muse A2
Prose Work VII

There's something almost uncanny about his creamy skin, too smooth and too soft to be entirely human. His hidrosis harbors nothing bitter; there is sugar is his swelter.
His groans, melodic. His gasps, a song. The way his brows come together when his lips part, when he comes undone, too symmetrical and too concerted to be pure reaction, or un-orchestrated.
But he's so fragile in his flesh; so small within the sheets.
Cradled by pale pink satin, lying on his back, he looks so thin, so delicate, so under my control. An arm extending upward, bent loosely at his elbow, hand turned toward his tussled hair, fingers unfurling, opening his palm to me.
The other arm bends, too. In my vision, it rests across his small waist; the hand hanging limply from the bent wrist. In my brain's interpretation, he is sheltering himself; not from me but from my impulse, my enthusiasm, the itch to make tender skin ache.
I can see his navel beneath his forearm. Above it are the bones of his rib cage, a perfect path for my fingertips to tread, until they find his nipple, soft and somewhat swollen, red; still glistening with my spit.
If I concentrate closely enough, I can see his heart

pounding at his chest.
Though his body's natural mechanisms work
quickly, roughly, rapidly, he seems to lay in rest. His
features are serene. He seems to pay no heed to the
places where he bleeds.
Beneath thick but orderly brows, flesh has softly
closed over glistening pearls of the purest white
adorned with sapphire cores.
The plump, pink lips are smiling, even as sharp
hiccups of serrated breath strangle his steady
inhalation. In tandem with his gasps, his muscles
tense. His small abdomen flexes as my nails run
over his ribs.
And I must be ovulating because the scent of his
sweat is divine. The sugar-water lingers on his lip,
cascades salt along his throat. His Adam's Apple
quivers, prompting another droplet to fall.
I gaze down to him, straddling his thighs, my knees
pressing into the silky pink sea encompassing him.
A reverse genuflection of the ascended to the
reposed.
He sighs. Eyes flutter open below the curve of
sympathetic brows. I can't tell if he's comfortable
or if he's afraid, if he's aroused or vibrating with the
adrenaline he'd need to try and flee.
I want to suffocate him in silk.
I want to watch him gasp and moan. I want to see
his back arching. My brain translates the images. I
am alive. On fire.

Vulnerable Boy

I whisper the words
The sweet nothings
Of pillow talk

Fully clothed
Unopened
And close

The blues of his irises
Swallowed by salt

For the praises remind him
Of nothing at all

He denies all my claims shyly
With blush in his cheeks

Responding with wordless lips
Through soft embraces

I accept and allow this

Offering in return
Gentle bites

Instead of more poetry
Leaving my lips

Either way
My affection is accurate
Because I've always
Loved through my teeth

POETRY OF THE REFLECTIVE MUSES

No Way to Identify Me

I watch Dead Poets Society
And I read Fight Club
And authors call these Stories for Men
But I feel more in tune with them
Than anything with Sisterhood in the title

I suppose it's because I seek freedom
I want to breathe free air
And exhale art
I want to escape capitalism
I want to hit things
I want to be a god

Why do people think
All women want is friends
And a push-up bra
And a cute a boy to kiss

I want to woo gentle men
With words
To circulate my sensual thoughts
Into their veins
So when they gasp and groan beneath me
They forget all other names and sensations
But "God, my God" and the divinity of my
embrace

I want these gentle men
To sit sideways on satin sheets
I want a ruby-red robe to hang loosely at their
waists
While its sleeve cascades around their arm
And reveals the skin of their shoulders

I want to gaze into their pretty faces
Stare into their eyes
And recite rhyme and syntax
Directly into their heart

I want my lies to trickle
Into vulnerable ears
So when their brains interpret what I say
They think it's all sincere

Am I male
Or am I female
Am I neither
Am I nothing

Perhaps I'm just a personality
Attracted to minds
Who will submit
Theirs souls,
And their flesh
to me

Nonfiction

Sometimes at night
Memories occur
Of the tangible reality
I've lived
And the visions are merely visions
And in the third person
I view myself
At a table
Or in a car
Or a stadium
Or convention hall
And I am not inside the body
Which acts as I had acted
Or sees what I had seen
I am but a character
Inside a living dream
When I think of who I was
During some of these events
I do not recognize the person
I do not feel like she exists
I do not think she is me
Merely some soul
Passing through this brain
Because when I think of all she was
I know we're not the same
Sometimes I think the weight
Of actions and words
Never really hit me

You Never Marry

Because it wasn't me
Inside the world
Then I wonder really
If I keep this realm at a distance
Not on purpose
Or by product
Of some fear or hate
But merely my disinterest
Other worlds are in my head
They're in my mind
My heart
My lap
Full of humans I could love
Full of poetics to consume
I wonder if I hate this plane we're in
Because better ones exist
And perhaps I would not be
So detached from supposed reality
If I weren't so attached to falsities
To lies
And words
And beauty
But having tasted idealism
Gives this realm its own flavor
Stale and rotten and distasteful
Full of cheap thrills
And pedestrian prose
It's why I'd rather spend
My time in solidarity
Meditating

Silent
Alone
Until some soul slips through the veil
Dividing two realities
And allows me access
To a world
Through that same third-party sight
That I can live in
That I can love
That I can write

No Confession Found

He says I can twist
His own words
To fit my point
And that it makes too much sense
For him to argue
I used to think
It was my way with words
My analysis of language
Then I thought
Perhaps
It was overthinking mixed
With those interpretation skills
But when I see their faces
I start to concede
That I may have abilities
That seem abusive
And like my love of language
I've never consciously used them
If this is just the way my brain functions
Is it me that's the monster
Or is it my mind
For no one can pinpoint the source
Of a thought

Don't Get in a Car with a Creative

He says I'm risking his life
When I text and drive
I ask if he thinks I care about his
More than I care about mine

The words that I type
Aren't just words to another

In folders and email drafts
They're the worlds I discover

They're the air in my lungs
The meat of my brain
The flick of my tongue
The blood in my veins

When they ignite from nothing
In the backdrop of my mind
I become substantial
I become defined

And if I don't allow it flow
When it rises to the tide
Then the life within this flesh of mine
Dies with the unborn lives inside

So I may risk his life
In this car with my phone

                    You Never Marry

But if I watch the road
instead of writing
The life I risk
is my own

Muse No. P

It's always so thrilling discovering the existence
of some attractive human
Because it reminds you
no matter
how many beautiful men you know
and see
and want to own
That there are countless others just as desirable
You don't know their names
You don't their faces
But they are existing
Out of sight and out of mind
out of awareness
God
I want to meet you
I wish I could watch you through my phone
If I could see you laugh or dance or sing
Without you knowing
Without either of us knowing
That we belong to one another
And that we'll know it someday

PrivTrau

When I was twenty six or twenty seven
A facialist dragged razors over my skin
During one treatment
She scraped at the flesh
Wrapped around my jawbone
And cut it open
Nothing deep
Nothing painful
Only scrapes;
A brush burn
The serrated skin formed scabs
Eventually
And it healed without a scar
But in the moment
She called it "good trauma"
And it made me remember
Being fifteen or sixteen
And using the pin of an old rusty broach
To carve words into my skin
I didn't use razors
Or blades
Nothing big
Nothing swift
I liked the smallness of the needle
Its precision
But mostly I liked to dig at my flesh
To watch the layers unfurl from the whole
Curling and thin

And wait eagerly to see
How many scratches it would take
To make myself bleed
Hunched over my body
I stared at my art
Digging and scraping
Slowly and watchful
Until flesh tones became pink
Then pink dotted red
Then I'd scratch further and further
Until I genuinely bled
My parent gagged the first time
The sleeve of my band shirt revealed one of my
words
So I learned to carve my writing
Into the skin covering the connection
Of leg and groin
Where the seam of my underwear
Rested against my left leg
A secret sacrament
Of skin and sentiment
I filled my ears with safety pins
But never shoved one through
I'd sit before the mirror for hours
Pressing the point against my skin
And circling it,
Circling it,
Circling it,
Until it broke through
Layer by layer

                              You Never Marry

Circling, circling, circling
A little deeper,
A slow pressure
A little further,
A slower push
Little by little
Layer by layer
Until it pierced through
Now my ear is full of hoops
Stamped .925 and shining
And the arm of my first carving
Is covered in tattoos
And the white scar letters are buried by black
Sometimes I forget they're even there
No one else knows that they are
But I still love the feeling
Of slow moving needles
And slow healing scabs

I Am Dyer

You wanted to navigate me
Silently and in secret
Like the slow and subtle turn of a wheel guiding a
metallic vessel along the course an increasingly
winding road
But there is no cartography to my soul
My veins are not roadways
Through which you can travel home
I am not so predictable
As a carbon copy artery
What you find within the flesh of others
You'll find has never been a part of me
I am not defined as concretely
As the synthetically conquered road
 Nor am I even as solid
As abandoned pathways reclaiming with nature
humanly-crafted stone
I am liquid can't you see?
My strength is not a rock on which you should lean
It'll chip and fragment and wear away
Until someone else replaces your gleam
You cannot predict the madness
Of a heart bereft of long term love
Residing there is only passion
Which ignites as abruptly as it dies
You cannot counter this expire because
With your manipulation or your lies
For I am not the stars

There is no pattern to my gleam
Remember that the galaxies are on fire
And their suffocating heat is what causes their
sheen
You won't navigate the swirling indentations of my
brain
You won't flow within my veins
You are a beautiful fragment of my existence
A fleeting memory of sunshine following a
cleansing rain

Weak in the Knees

There is not much weakness.
Inside me is strength.
I am not only confident,
But arrogant,
Arguably to a dangerous point.
I like to be right.
I'll fight to the death.
Die on a hill.
Before I concede to anything.
The moment someone suggests something
I was already planning to do
I suddenly lose all desire to do it.
And if someone suggests, even slightly implies
That I shouldn't do something
I perform it innumerable times.
I'm stubborn
I'm selfish
I'm egocentric
And bold
I'm pretentious
I'm combative
Aggressive
And loud
I'm boisterous
I'm harsh
I crave all attention
Scared of commitment
Your terms

    You Never Marry

Having standards
In mine
Immature
Well, perhaps
I don't want kids
I love my cats
And I'll love them more
Than any human caller
Pregnancies sicken me
Babies are leeches
When I see fetus kicks
I recoil in odium
The only thing worse than being called someone's
wife
Would be being called someone's mother
But I only wear dresses
I like makeup and drag
It's easy access to an unbreakable wall
So know that if you're pretty
If you're skinny
If you're meek
I'll fall in love with you in a second
Because only fragility can make me weak

Calling You Perfect is so Clichéd:
Adoration, Idolatry, and Platonic Love of a Solemn
Charmer

Let's make a sequel
To a life we never lived

Let's see if our eternity
Is only relative

Let's inject into our veins
All the glory of the skin

And hold inside our hearts
The danger setting in

I want to taste the honey
Coating words across your tongue

So when you give to me your essence
I won't fully come undone

Let me dig my nails so deeply
They embed inside your flesh

And rip away from fingers
Writing words within the mess

Your blood is sweet and tender
You hold sugar in your spit

You house within your fingers
An inability to miss

Feel me solid and congealed
As I gush upon your brain

So when I feel you firm and taut
I can think the same

I want to hear your gasping
As you articulate the groans

For nothing is as sexual
As a king upon his throne

He whispers words of praise
While instructing secretly

So when we fall onto knees
We think the choice was free

I recognize desire
Inside the hefty home

A fleshy cell of confirmation
That his soul's a catacomb

The sinews and the jagged veins
Are corridors to roam

The pulpit at the center
Where his mind has overgrown

The intellect spews from him
Like a kiss exchanging spit

A ritual of reason
Inside an endless pit

What will we name the novel
Of our trilogies of sin

The evidence of sorrow
Upon the rigid chin

Lips like bows blow open
Loosening the chord

No need to try to conquer
What you've already allured

My praise is so platonic
It reveals a danger through

Every single adjective
My mind decides to spew

He's perfect
He's perfect

                    You Never Marry

He's perfect
He's whole

If I didn't know him
I'd want to overthrow him

Own his flesh
And then his soul

Visitor

I hear the phrase people say across the seas;
I see the hand gestures commonly offered in place
of a common wave.
I have been to both places;
I have breathed foreign air.
I have spoken words on airplanes
To strangers
With jobs I didn't even know existed.
I have traveled with my family,
With my friends,
I have traveled alone.
But I have never spent significant time away from
my front porch.
I have never left my cats for more than two weeks
at one time.
I have seen things,
I have heard things,
I have touched things,
Far beyond the Three Rivers of my round-up city,
But I have never lived further than thirty minutes,
From the house where I grew up.
I have learned,
I have listened,
But I have never been immersed.
I have been a visitor here.
I have been a visitor everywhere.
A student,
A seeker,

A wanderer,
But only by visitation.

My Friend, the Musician;
Not a Muse, but a Teacher

He sits
In the passengers seat of my car
And asks if he can use my charger
I tell him he can
And watch what's mine enter what is his
He looks over to me with his phone in his hand
A smirk slipping across lips
Dying to speak
A twinkle in his eye as his brows raise
"Want to hear an unreleased song?"
He asks
As if I'd say no
He warns about that's it raw, that it's crude
Tells me nothing's mixed or mastered
As if he doesn't understand
That what I love most about him
Is the beauty of his thoughts
Unprocessed
In their truest form
For the purity of his soul
In the roughness of the art unedited
Unrestrained and unembellished
Exposed
Before the mask
Covers his spirit just enough
To keep us all
At arm's length

Cockiness in Two Forms:
The Brain and The Body

I don't want to be anything but a brain
But my brain interprets what I see
And when I look in the mirror
I struggle with what's reflected back to me
It's not insecurity that radiates inside the frame
I genuinely like what I see
Which causes a strange sensation of shame
I want to take my photo
I want to share my skin
But every time I almost do
I'm reminded of the fleshy sin
I don't want someone to see me
And tell me that I'm hot
I want to be the manifestation
And everything it's not
I want to be the mind
Behind the flashy eyes
I want to be soul
Buried deep within my thighs
I want to wear lace bottoms
And nothing but a half top
Yet the idea of being attractive
Puts it to a halt
If I can't be respected
While revealing hints of skin
Then I don't want to be a body
Only what resides within

Mortality

So entranced with new and better and improved
We replace our phones as frequently as the
calendar comes down
Allowing space for a new year of blocks
Our limited time awaiting
New releases
While old books rot on the shelves
New movies
While discs host dust upon the shelves
A tape replaced by a disk
The disk replaced by yet another
Car companies release updated versions
Of the same model with each fallen year
We watch videos of junkyards destroying
What once was newest and most elite
Maps replaced with systems
Rendered obsolete by the same technology
Embedded in those phones
That never stay with us for more than a year or
two
And we must erase the contents of our closest
For brand new cotton-poly blends and imitation
silk
Jeans that still fit
Get thrown in bins
While we fill basket with their replacements
Delighting in the smell of something new
Eager to experience something different

And yet we wonder
Why God
Doesn't let His creations
Live forever

Sticky Lashes

I'm awake in last night's makeup
I didn't go anywhere
I didn't 'party'
I slept in my own bed
By myself
Sober
At 10 pm
I thought about washing the mascara from my
lashes
Considered splashing water on my face
Old sunscreen still caught in all the creases
Old memories still caught in the subconscious
I could step into the shower
Couldn't bring myself to wash my hair
And everything's fine
Everything's perfect
The only reason for my exhaustion
Is the chemical production in my brain
Erase the memories
Produce serotonin
Not so I can sleep
Or find peace
But so I can find the strength to wash my face

The Human Portrayal

I press my heels into the icy snow
As they carry
All one hundred
Thirty pounds
Of me
To a car
Without four wheel drive
My slacks are black
My shirt is gray
Its sleeves cover
My tattoos
But its v-shaped neck
Would reveal breasts
If I had larger ones
And its bottom hem
Is too short for my torso
So my midriff is exposed
Not only to the frigid air
For my jacket has one button
And blows open
But also
The the eyes of those
Judging me for unprofessional attire
While they lick their lips
And don't make eye contact
With me
I spent three days
In the same shirt

Sleeveless and loose
The trappings of civilization
Shucked off
Tossed
Into a pile of polyester and cotton
On my bedroom floor
I ran a brush through my hair
And hit a snag
Reaching for it
I removed a bobby-pin
I forget was even there
I wonder how many nights
I slept on its metal
Never knowing
It was embedded in my unwashed hair
An actor is glamour
A rock star is grunge
But these displays
Mean nothing to
A writer
Who wraps intellect in emotion
And seals it with purple prose
All while they sip cold coffee
From a rinsed out mug
Wearing dirty clothes

Generous

It's not all take
I give and I provide
All the pleasure with the pain
Occurring when we collide
The two frames mangled
High-speed amorous wreck
Wrapped around each other
As I lick the sweat from your neck
Sink my teeth into your flesh
After kissing it gently
When you recoil I pull you against me
Offering you the warmth and wetness
Of my mouth and my lips
With the tender pets to your hair
And the friction of hips
You groan and gasp
Succumbing to me
Pliant at last
Your hands rising
Reaching for me
Holding my back
Drawing me in
As I draw from your skin
The lifeforce iron and red
Pushing at your shoulders
Until you sink into the bed
Slip away from this world
Feel the fantasy of sin

While I tear into your flesh
And draw your body in
Swallowing you whole
Flesh and blood fulfilling me
Lost in my complete control
You've never felt more free
My tongue brushes over your clavicle
Nerve endings ignite in these sins of the flesh
Affectionately disguised as a miracle
Hands slipping down your chest
Nails digging into the frame
As it unfurls in curling rivulets
The markings of my claim
When you shout out my name
You gasp an anagram
Speaking in tongues
See what a generous god I am
Gripping you tightly
Marbling the sky of your flesh
As if the shape of my prints
Were constellations on the sky
Of your skin

I whisper calming words when you start cry
When the pain overwhelms all the pleasure
And your climax subsides
Lulling you back into comfort
With the silver tongue inside my teeth
That's as sharp as it is slippery
A metamorphosis occurs

On the silver tongue inside my teeth
Its slippery surface grows sharp
As the lullaby slips into eulogy
Drawing you into the secret garden
Where the satin of our bed
Becomes the lining of a box

There's nothing more dangerous
Than the silent killer in your bed
Who stole the heart in your chest
Inside the brain your head

My Muse; Mine

He says I'm obsessive,
He says rabid, feral,
Disturbingly lovestruck.
But I just simply cannot fathom
Being inspired by something
I can't fuck.
I want to own what ignites the soul.
Breathe it in,
And let it out.
So when it leaves it's only by expression,
For its essence stays within me,
When I'm holy and devout.
And when I feel its fires burning
When flames roll across my skin
I release it from my rib cage
Touch its chest
And grip its hips
And urge back within.
When he gasps his poetry
His spirit soaks my brain
While I soak his thighs and hips
With my own encompassing motion
Of effort, time, attention,
Lust, and spit.
He thinks I want him always
But if he leaves I'm fine
The only thing that can't retreat
Is an act performed

In any way, especially
The collision of body heat
So my end goal
Is always the same pressure
The same experience
Of love and leisure
It is not hedonistic
It is not lust or greed or immorality
It's merely ensuring I own some piece of him
He cannot take back from me

THE LENGTHY

Leo Cusp

I lie awake in bed
Just waiting for daybreak
Because my body's exhausted
But my mind is wide awake

Sometimes I stare at my hands
Wondering what my fingers can do
I can hold a knife as easily as a pen
With either grip
I can murder you

And the thought rushes my body
And I feel my heart in my ears
All bodily motions enmesh
While my lungs are divided
By a freezing line of ice
In the center of my chest

Blood boils
But the heart turns cold
So when the heat meets the frost
It cracks and shatters
And the blood splatters
And my satin sheets
Look a massacre
Occurred
While you laid there fast asleep

Never moving,
Counting sheep
While I cut myself so deep
The carbon dioxide
From your unconscious exhales
Creeps into me
Seeps into me
Stifling my skin
Where I bleed

You're a healer
A cold-heart stealer
A drug dealer
A poet
Lacing lies
With honesty
Too horrible to admit
In any plain way
So we speak in metaphor
Because you're too soft for my gore
And I'm too hard for your velour
Skin like velvet
Soul like down

I grab at your arms
Watching my fingerprints
As they rise beneath the surface
Of your skin
A claim on the creamy flesh
Five bruises tender and fresh

May seem like a curse
But it's how I bless
What I intend to possess
Because I adore you
I obsess
And it's not enough to profess
I confess
My love for you
Encourages me to oppress
While you express
Such distress
Such protest
It's playful though
And I know your type
Well enough to know
You fight
To maintain the facade
Of a righteous god
But I'm the only divinity
In this parted sea
Of lips and thighs
Of hips and sighs

So I squeeze more tight
While your "no"s indict
Me for everything excit-
ing me in this moment
Of pitch black night
A little lamb lying down with a lion
A murderer deciding to write

A confession while you're dying
To break away
From the possessive hold
Digging into the display
Of dignity you've sold

But you can't escape me
And you don't want to
You want to flaunt through
The story while I haunt you

And I love to be villain
Make me into the bad guy
It's your story; write me in
Tell them how you want to die
How I force you
How I make you cry
How you could've broken away from me
How you could've just fled
How when you back away from me
It's toward the edge of my bed

So I can throw you into satin
Tear off your polyblend armor
So it's just my eyes devouring your skin
And your innocent allure
You're too pure
To engage with me in sin
Regardless you lust
And you trespass

You commit
Because this kind of injury
You admit
Feels sweeter when the one who delivers
Is the one who kisses it

I rectify
You deify

Replacing a lifetime of hurt
With the kind of pain you deserve
Expressed without reserve
The desires that unnerve
The sober mind
Lost behind
The love drunk awareness
Of you and me and this bareness
This rawness between us
Your submission
My control
The vulnerability of both your body
And your soul

When we sin
You take my name in vein
Groaning blasphemous
Praises in reverence
When it's finished
You can't flee
Can't run from me

Can't hide
Even when the rapture subsides

They think you're weak
Because you're shy
Because you're meek
And you're a guy

But you stare up at me
In the darkness encompassing
Everything you see
And the fire in my eyes
Is the inferno in my soul
I don't need to go to hell
I'm the devil in my role
As the liar
The corruption
Your situation's dire
Because you're here
For my consumption

But there's no fear in your veins
Like what runs through their eyes
When they look at me
Because you lie down next to me
Knowing you could die

Knowing you might never wake up
Depending on which personality
Rises to the surface of this body I call 'me'

Because multiple souls exist in this skin
And most of them killers
Executed from the earth
And dying to get back in

Through lust and violence
I write everything they put at a distance
But it's near and dear
To everything you fear
And you don't reach for your clothes
You don't run when I juxtapose
Everything sick and morose
With the poetics you love most
We lay utterly engrossed
In everything we boast
Everything we suppose
Until we diagnose
One another as a host
Of unholy chaos

But no righteous or wrong exist in my realms
Only desire, lust, and power with me at the helms
Of both my body and your own
As you gasp and groan
You give it away
Your skin and soul

I'll devour you
Come into me
Let me wash away your tears

                    You Never Marry

While I tear into your brain

The ice in my veins
The heat on the lips
The thoughts in my brain
The motion of hips

What do you feel internally
When I slice you open physically
Do you gasp for a reprieve
From the fire that you breathe
Burning your lungs
Igniting your flesh and bone
Or do you delight in the pain of submitting
Of being mine and owned

This god isn't righteous
I delight in your crisis
And when you're mindless
When you're spineless
That's when you're most pious

Left to my vices
Breathe me in
Bow your head
My bloody sacrifice
Scratched up skin
Drink of me
Eat of my flesh
Amen

Marble Man

A statuesque Adonis
Will always decay
Even the granite of his body
Will crack and crumble and fade away

His eyes lose their gleam
He lowers his strong chin
The lovely marble of his frame
Becomes soft, tender skin

The brittle bones break
The creamy flesh thins
And every force outside him
Overpowers the spirit within

As his knees grow weaker
He falls from his pillar
The silence of the ticking clock
The unforgiving killer

Collapsed on the ground
Wings thrown about his head
He melts into the satin
Of his eternal bed

I stand over him
Gazing down at the alchemy

                    You Never Marry

Watching chiseled stone
Become the confines of humanity

I grab at his arms
Jerk him upward toward me
He blinks, slowly opens his eyes
Looks up, imploringly

He's alluring
Through all he's endured
The breaks in his stone
Reveal the skin it obscured

Cured by the earth's clay
Where he lies
Reaching for the pillar
As he tries

To rise
To his feet
To ascend
The concrete

Now rendered obsolete
By his fall to the ground
Inside the earthen gravity
To which he's bound

His knees buckle again
He reaches to the skies

As he plummets to the planet
He collides roughly and cries

That he doesn't want to die
I tell him he's fine, he's alive
For the first time
He lifts a granite hand and sighs

You know, he says
You can't deny
The moment we start to live
Is the moment we start to die

If I remained solid
Concrete marble
I wouldn't have existed
But I wouldn't have to crumble.

His fingers curl inward
Toward his palm into a fist
The marble busting open from the motion
Breaking loose his knuckles and his wrist

He sits up and gasps
Staring at the revealed skin
His voice shakes and rasps
As he whispers, its so thin

It's so fragile
It can be ripped and cut and torn

                    You Never Marry

I tell him not to be so hostile
From broken granite, he was born

But marble has no nerve
He points out to me
That flesh signals pain to the brain
When it bleeds

But when granite falls apart
There is no carnage
Granite has no brain or heart
No veins to burst and hemorrhage

But stone cannot feel
I counter this claim
Through frigid snow and raging heat
It remains entirely the same

It does not change
It does shiver or sweat
Another benefit, he says
That weather poses no threat

No object holds regret
He continues with conviction
That temperature had no effect
But on flesh imposes great affliction

A small sacrifice, I say
Reaching for him again

For flesh is the only thing
That can feel warm skin

What when it dies, he asks
Eyes gazing at our connection
Watching nerve ending burst
With this lively infection

Then you return here
I say, your eternity restored
When you're buried in the earth
Beneath the marble you adore

When the flesh rots away
Your bones will remain
Forever they'll lie here
In sun and snow and rain

He counters forlornly
That death destroys permanence
His features twist in understanding
In the loss of innocence

So what is it you fear
I ask with intrigue
That you'll feel, that you'll hurt
Or that you'll cease to be

All of it he says
Everything about being

Cannot be enjoyed
When you know it's so fleeting

Then lie back into the snow
I say turning away
Freeze and turn to stone
And rush to decay

But no he shakes
He trembles in fear
I cannot die alone
I cannot die here

So live I offer
And extend my hand
Go into mortality
Death be damned

And what of heaven
He asks what of hell
Best not to consider I say
Until that final farewell

He purses his lips
And more stone falls away
I don't want to exist he says
Because I don't want to decay

But if it's inevitable
I suppose

I'll try to embrace it
Before I repose

He looks to the pillar
One final time
And bids farewell to his life
As he walks into mine

BREVITY

Call Me Your Master

Some call me Satan,
But some call me The Christ.
Come into my arms, little angel,
As a willing sacrifice.
I'll bleed you of your sanctity,
Delude you in a rapturous sin,
We'll withdraw from you the spirit,
Leave you wrapped in wounded skin.

Poem XVIII

I feel the stars igniting in my mind
I feel the worms at my feet

Galaxies bloom inside me
While the maggots slip into my soul

I throw up static
I exist in a hole

And every time I feel pain
They feed me a treat

Breaded

I feel the flutter in my chest
Rattling the rib cage
Tearing open the flesh
Splitting me in two
The hole where my heart should be
Spreads through the muscle
Ripping through the veins
Devouring the organs
Hollowing out my form
Until I'm nothing more
Than a skeleton
Wrapped in skin

Mind Mirror

Sometimes I wish I had amnesia
So I could forget everything I've ever written
And then sit down with a pot of coffee
And some oat milk
And my cats
And read my work
Just to see
What I'd really think of me
If I weren't inside this body
With this brain attached
To my soul

Tangible Unknowing

I see you and I want to cry
I hear you and I feel the tingling
I think I want you
I don't know you
Not in this life
Not like I want to
And I wonder
If I want to know you now
Because you're mine somewhere else

Temple Down - Small Cage

I feel my pulse in my ears
My thoughts in my veins
I breathe through my heart
Love with my teeth
When I whisper words
It's with my fingertips
And when I offer affection
It resides in my ribs
My muscles stretch
Until my eyes detach
Nerves become nothing
Blood becomes ash

Temple Down - Large Cage

The walls shake
The house trembles with fear
The floor quakes
Foundations break
The end is near

Carpet unfurls
Littering the atmosphere
Wallpaper curls
Objects are hurled
The end is here

Beyond Doubt

I want to hear the sounds of your inner monologue.
I want to hear your voice when it exists in your
mind.
I want to see thing words unspoken.
Know what no one can ever know.
I wouldn't believe your words
The way I'd believe your soul
I want to hear your thoughts.
I want to know.
Not think
Or interpret
Or be told.
I want to know.

THE ONLY LOVE POEM
I'VE EVER WRITTEN

MK & ICK

I can't count the amount of times
I've wished for a car to slam into mine,
to total it, to catch it on fire,
with me still inside.

I have visions
Every time a car passes by
And I grip tightly my wheel in reality
Encouraged by the hallucination
Of a potential future
For a could flick my wrist
And it would all be over.

I like to borrow money
From all my wasted time
To see how much my misery is worth
How many objects
Commodities
Could my soul be worth

I'd rather die sometimes

But I don't want to be a poet
Who is appreciated a century
After her skin has rotted
Away from the skull
That once held the brain
That crafted these stanzas

                    You Never Marry

These novels
These thoughts.

So I don't jerk my wheel into oncoming traffic
I follow the invisible lines
Down synthetic roads
And stop when blinking lights
Tell me so

All these signals
All these regulations
All these careers
All these educations

The illusion
Of choice
Leads us so often
To making the wrong ones

Perhaps dying wouldn't be wrong
For we all must do it
But destroying the machinery
Of a detestable species
Feels very, very
Right…eous
And correct

Besides contemplation
And morality
And life

And all its supposed glory

The only thing keeping me
With absolutely certainty
Upon this track
Is the fact that my cats,
If I veered to the left into death,
Would keep waiting for me to come back

POETRY OF THIS BOOK'S APOCALYPSE

I Don't Want to Make You Immortal

I've wasted so many words on some souls
I swore I'd never turn into prose
Because even when people die
Our creations don't

Poem V

Every time I fall in love
I experience such profound sadness
Because I know I'll never love
the object of my affection
As intensely as I do in that moment
of conscious attachment
With knowledge comes truths
That are never as pretty as lies
Especially the ones we conjure
In the thrill of the vision's potential
In our minds

The End

They recount the evil-doers
The militant and elected
And they make sure to say
The third one
Will be a 'he' like they
But I don't think
The antichrist
Is one of borders to reign
I think she is a person, instead
Who knows how to control the brain
She'll seduce a kingdom
With her words and with her prose
Seeping into their consuming minds
All the thoughts on this vast world
And they won't know they've succumbed
Their surrender is not so overt
As uninhibited actions
Dressed in uniform to gloat
The leaders of the world
Will unite against her

And when they ban her books
She'll sing songs to the masses
When the rhythm's banned
She'll film the tales
They tried to stop her from telling
She'll use art and entertainment to disguise what
she is selling
She is written in the stars
Made of prophecy and prose
And while they submit in their subconscious
She'll be the only one who knows
That she is incarnate
She is evil
She is master
She is lethal
Because a man can be killed
A bomb can be detonated
But an idea is forever
A thought cannot be assassinated

Index

Other Works by Brooklynn

The Woman in Red Heels
The Word of the Rock God
Fiberglass Galaxy
Amethyst
2288

The Anti-Gospels
Deification *(Book I)*
Grieving the Spirit *(Book II)*
Dead Works *(Book III)*
Famulus Falsus *(Book IV)*

Remember that readers love reviews.
Leave an honest one somewhere online.
xx

www.ingramcontent.com/pod-product-compliance
Lightning Source LLC
Chambersburg PA
CBHW021002160726

47994CB00006B/2336